SURFING

by Ben Mondy

ticktock

The author

Ben Mondy was lucky enough to grow up near Redhead Beach, a well-known surfing spot on the east coast of Australia. He started surfing in his early teenage years and, by the time he was 15, had decided that surfing was to be his major passion in life.

With thanks to: Diana LeCore, Sarah Jones and Tim Sanders

Thank you to Lorraine Petersen and the members of nasen

ISBN-13: 978 1 84898 143 0 pbk
This revised edition published in 2010 by *ticktock* Media Ltd

Printed in China
9 8 7 6 5 4 3 2 1

Copyright © *ticktock* Entertainment Ltd 2008, 2010
First published in Great Britain as *Xtreme Sports* in 2008 by *ticktock* Media Ltd,
103 Goods Station Road, Tunbridge Wells, Kent, TN1 2DP

Picture credits (t=top; b=bottom; c=centre; l=left; r=right; OFC=outside front cover):
ACM Writing Group: 7t, 10, 15bl, 21tr, 21cl, 28, 39cr, 39b, 42, 43b. Simon Adams: 43t. Buzz Pictures/Alamy: 11b, 31t. Getty Images: 54, 55b. Tim Jones: 34, 50, 51t, 51b. Ben Mondy: 12/13. Nordicphotos/Alamy: 30. O'Neill: 4/5, 46/47t. Kirk Owers: 57t. Peterson: 9b. Quicksilver: 6, 7b, 20t, 36/37, 44/45, 56. Rip Curl: 52/53. Shutterstock: OFC, 3, 8t, 17 all, 32t, 38, 39t, 39cl. Tracks: 60/61b. Tropicalpix: 48. Henrik Trygg/Corbis: 19cr. www.aspworldtour.com: 11t, 14/15t, 14b, 16, 18, 19t, 19cl, 19b, 24, 26/27t, 26b, 27bl, 27br, 31b, 33t, 33b, 35t, 35b, 41t, 41cr, 46b, 47b, 49, 55t, 55c, 57b, 58t, 58b, 59t, 59b. www.shortyphotos.com: 1, 25t, 25b, 41cl, 41b. www.swillyphotos.com: 2, 15br, 40. www.hotstuffpictures.com: 22/23, 29tr, 29cl.

Every effort has been made to trace copyright holders, and we apologize in advance for any omissions. We would be pleased to insert the appropriate acknowledgments in any subsequent edition of this publication.

CONTENTS

CHAPTER 1: INTRODUCTION

US surfer Corey Lopez carves through the face of a wave. It takes great strength and skill to master waves.

OVERVIEW

Surfing has been around for many years. It is one of the most fantastic sports on the planet.

Kelly Slater

Lifestyle

Surfing is much more than a healthy, fun sport. Surfing is a way of life.

Travel

Surfers travel for miles to surf, talk to surfers and surf different kinds of waves.

Surfers are always trying to improve.

A surfer performs a fast turn on a wave.

HISTORY OF SURFING

The Hawaiian people enjoyed surfing almost 1,000 years ago. When the first Europeans arrived in Hawaii in the late 1700s, surfing almost died out.

Then, just over 100 years ago, some old surfboards were found and surfing was rediscovered.

A memorial dedicated to Duke Kahanamoku

1907 – George Freeth becomes the first surfer in California, USA.

1915 – Duke Kahanamoku introduces surfing to Australia.

1957 – Surfing is introduced in France by American Peter Viertel.

1958 – One of the best waves in the world, Supertubes, is discovered in South Africa.

Travelling is a part of surfing.

In the early 1900s, Olympic swimming champion Duke Kahanamoku helped revive surfing in Hawaii.

1961 – Australian Peter Troy introduces surfing to Brazil.

1971 – Australian Steve Cooney rides the 4.5-metre-high Uluwatu wave in Bali, Indonesia.

TYPES OF SURFING

There are three main types of surfing: short boarding, long boarding and tow surfing.

A short-board surfer performs a perfect snap turn.

Short boarding

Short boarding is the most common form of surfing. Short boarders perform a number of different turns on and above the waves. The boards are usually about two metres long.

10

Long boarding

In long boarding, the surfers let the waves direct them. The surfboards, sometimes called Malibus, are longer and heavier than short boards.

Tow surfing

Tow surfing involves surfers getting towed by a rope behind a jet ski.

Tow surfing is usually used for very large waves.

No need to paddle with tow surfing!

CHAPTER 2: GEAR

AND FASHION

Surfers watch the breaking waves as one of them waxes up his surfboard. Surfers need a surfboard, wetsuit, leg rope and wax. Then, they are ready to surf.

TYPES OF BOARD

The most popular board is the short board. But there are many different boards in all shapes and sizes.

A long board is thicker, heavier and more stable than a short board.

A long board is more difficult to turn. Long boards have a wide nose.

Surfers 'hang' their toes off the end.

14

A tow board is towed into big waves by a powered craft. A tow board has feet straps.

The fish is easy to paddle.

A fish is shorter than a short board but is much wider and thicker. A fish is designed for very small waves.

A tow board is small but heavy.

ANATOMY OF A SURFBOARD

A surfboard can be broken down into four main parts: length, width, rails and fins.

Andy Irons inspects the damage done to the tail of his short board.

Surfers call a group of surfboards a quiver.

Nose

Length

Tail

Length

The length of the board is measured from the nose (front) of the surfboard to the tail (back).

Width

The width of the surfboard is measured at its widest point. This is usually halfway between the nose and tail.

Width

Rails

Rails

The rails are the curved edges of the surfboard that run from the nose to the tail.

Fins

The fins at the back of the board make it stable. Surfboards can have between one and four fins. The most popular is three fins (a tri-fin).

Fins

17

EQUIPMENT

Besides a surfboard, surfers need other gear. This gear includes a wetsuit, leg rope and wax.

Sofia Mulanovich grew up surfing in Peru in cold water. She always wears a full-length wetsuit.

SURFING

Wetsuit

A wetsuit is a rubber suit that keeps surfers warm in cold water.

Leg rope

The leg rope is a cord that connects a surfer's leg to the board. This stops surfers losing their boards when they fall off.

Wax

Surfboards are made out of fibreglass. Wax is rubbed on to the surface of the board to provide grip.

Deck grip

Deck grip

Deck grip is a pad that can be glued to a surfboard instead of using wax.
It provides traction (grip).

19

SURFING CULTURE

Surfing has had a major impact on the world outside of the water.

In the 1960s, The Beach Boys sang about surfing in their music. Today, Jack Johnson is popular for his surf music.

Surfer and musician Jack Johnson

Keanu Reeves and Patrick Swayze in the film Point Break

There is a huge interest in surfing from movies and TV.

Surfing fashion can be seen in shops around the world.

We use many words and phrases that started off in surfing. Here is a list of some of these words:

- wipe out
- dude
- going bananas
- cowabunga

CHAPTER 3: WAVES

Pro surfer Conan Hayes rides a towering tube wave breaking off the coast of Hawaii.

WAVES

BREAKING WAVES

Waves travel from way out in the deep ocean. They break when they reach shallower water.

How waves work

Waves break because the 'bottom' portion of the wave hits the shallow sand or reef.

The 'top' portion of the wave moves forward until the top portion falls over.

Flat sandy beaches that slope gently into the water have slow low-rise waves

Wave speed

The faster a wave travels from deep to shallower water, the faster the wave breaks. In Hawaii, waves come from deep in the Pacific Ocean and break very fast on the shallow reefs.

A series of three waves break off the coast of Mexico

Sets

Waves usually arrive in groups called sets. Sets can be three, four or five waves that arrive one after the other.

Sets are normally bigger than other waves. Some sets can include up to ten waves!

25

NAMES OF WAVES

A wave can be named after its geographic location, the way it breaks or the first person to surf it.

Beach breaks are waves that break over a sandy beach. They are not forceful.

Beach breaks can change from day to day as the sand moves.

At a beach break, the waves break in a random manner

Reef breaks are waves that break over a reef or rock. They are powerful and can be dangerous.

Point breaks are waves that wrap around a point or headland.

The famous Hawaiian wave Pipeline, breaking close to shore

Waves roll down a sandy point break in Australia

THE BEST WAVES

Jeffreys Bay in South Africa is considered to have some of the best waves in the world

There are surfers riding waves all around the world. The waves that break the best, longest or biggest become famous and attract surfers.

In surfing, waves are said to break either left or right. A wave is called a right-hander if, from a surfer's viewpoint, it travels towards the right. A left-hander is the opposite.

*Waves breaking on
a coral reef off the
coast of Fiji*

In Hawaii, the waves
are large and break
in shallow water.

Australia has a wide
range of waves.

In Indonesia, the
waves break in
perfect formation
over coral reefs.

*Australia has fun small
waves like this one.
It also has the towering
Cyclops wave.*

SURFING THE WORLD

Surfers travel the globe searching for exciting new places to surf.

In August 2007, the world's first glacial surf ride on Copper River, Alaska, USA, was recorded.

Kealii Mamala and Garrett McNamara caught the waves when a large iceberg broke off a glacier!

A surfer tackling the ice-cold Arctic waves off the coast of Norway

Wave freeze

New surfers thinking of travelling to Alaska or Iceland, beware! You'll need a thick wetsuit – the water there is only a few degrees above freezing.

Challenge

Despite travelling and competing around the world for over 15 years, former world champion Layne Beachley still loves Hawaii the best.

Layne Beachley surfing Sunset Beach, Hawaii

A surfer being wiped out by a massive wave off the island of Maui, Hawaii.

SCARY WAVES

Some professional surfers train their whole lives to surf big waves.

The scariest wave in the world is called Jaws. Jaws is located by the island of Maui in Hawaii. Jaws can break with a wave height of 24 metres!

Dungeons

A wave called Dungeons, near Cape Town in South Africa, is also very scary.

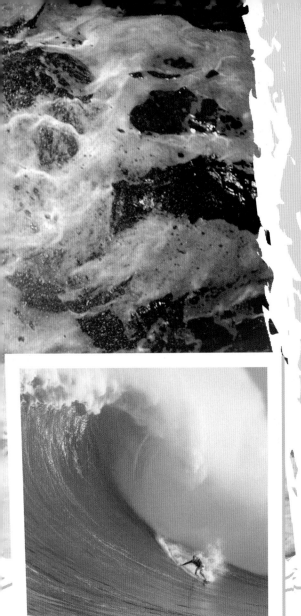

You can surf Jaws only by being towed in by a jet ski.

Jaws breaks over a sharp reef and ends on big cliffs with large and dangerous rocks.

The break of the Dungeons wave is not as big as Jaws, but it does break between one and two kilometres out to sea in freezing cold water.

SAFETY AND RULES

The powerful and changeable ocean makes surfing dangerous.

Sunset Beach, Hawaiii. The clear water in the middle of the beach is the rip going out to sea.

Rips

With waves constantly pushing water to the shore, sea water needs to return back to the open ocean.

It does this by travelling through deep channels on the ocean floor. These channels are called rips.

Sharks

The odds of a shark attack are fairly low.

In the 20th century, there were a total of between 30 and 75 shark attacks worldwide.

US surfer Bethany Hamilton was attacked by a shark at the age of 13 when surfing in Hawaii.

Two surfers get tangled up trying to work out who has the right of way.

Rules

There is an unwritten surfing code. This code says that the surfer who is already riding the wave, or who is paddling closest to the breaking part, has the right to surf that wave first.

CHAPTER 4: MOVES

AND STYLES

Professional surfer Ry Craike performs an aerial. A major part of surfing is about the radical 'turns' a surfer can perform. The best surfers in the world can perform huge jumps of over 1.8 metres.

THE BASIC MOVES

The first thing to figure out is how to stand on the board. You can either be a goofy footer or a regular (natural) footer.

A goofy surfs with the right foot forward.

A regular surfs with the left foot forward.

Paddle out

A surfer usually paddles out through the waves to the take-off zone.

Duck dive

A duck dive enables a surfer to go under an oncoming wave when paddling out.

Paddling

To get enough speed to catch a wave, it is important to do three or four quick paddling strokes just before the wave breaks.

Take-off

Professional surfers stand up at the very last second and take-off on the wave.

DIFFERENT MOVES

Once a new surfer has mastered the basics they can learn some different moves.

Tube

A tube is where a surfer is covered up by the lip of the wave and is locked inside.

Another name for a tube is a barrel.

Bottom-hand turn

This is the first move every surfer makes. The surfer leans over at the bottom of the wave after take-off and heads for the open face.

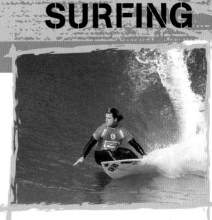

Re-entry

A basic move where the surfer turns on the top part of the wave before 're-entering' back down the face.

Cutback

After gaining speed on the open face, a surfer rides to the top of the crest. Then they cutback by turning the board toward the beach and then aiming back toward where the wave is breaking.

Aerial

This move became popular in the 1980s. The surfer and board leave the water, fly into the air and land.

KITE SURFING

The new sport of kite surfing has started to influence surfing.

Kite surfers leap into the air and perform moves up to 40 metres from the water's surface.

Twists

The use of a kite allows a surfer to generate more speed and to jump higher into the air.

Surfers can do more advanced twists and turns in the air.

Wind

A lot of surfers use both forms of surfing.
In strong winds, they kite surf and try new tricks.

When the wind dies down, the surfers return
to a normal board.

Speed

Kite-surfing experts can reach speeds of 80 kilometres per hour.

CHAPTER 5: THE FUTURE

OF SURFING

Surfers like Kelly Slater are responsible for pushing surfing to amazing new levels. The sport has also become incredibly popular. There are an estimated 20 million surfers worldwide.

A surfer rises at least 1.8 metres into the air above the ocean.

Taj Burrow gets ready to land. Burrow is one of the world's best aerial surfers.

AERIAL SURFING

More and more surfing is now being performed in the air above a wave, rather than on it. These moves are known as aerials. Top surfers can perform aerials three metres above the water!

2005 world champion Chelsea Georgeson gets speed to perform an aerial

Aerials involve the surfer spinning and trying to perform as many turns as possible in one go.

Complex moves such as a full somersault aren't yet possible.

A FlowRider in Malaysia

WAVE POOLS

One of the most successful wave-pool inventions is the FlowRider. The FlowRider is a standing wave that was designed by American Tom Lochtefeld.

A wave is created that stays in exactly the same position and at the same height.

Aerial specialist Josh Kerr

Surfers can perform the same turns in wave pools that they can on real waves.

HIGH WAVES

Wave face

Pete Cabrinha rides Jaws off the coast of Maui, Hawaii, which was measured at 21 metres

How high?

A wave is 21-metres high if the wave face is 21 metres high. Photographs and video footage are used to measure exactly how high the wave face is.

Surfer

*A surfer rides Ghost Trees in California,
which is famed for its big waves*

Wave waiters

There are always surfers waiting for the big waves to be discovered. The trick is finding where the waves are.

Big awards

The official world wave record stands at 21 metres.

This was a Jaws wave surfed by Pete Cabrinha in 2004.

The Rip Curl Pro, held at Bells Beach, Australia, is the longest-running professional surfing event in the world. It attracts 150,000 spectators every year.

IMPORTANT EVENTS

Surfing events are held for men, women and juniors. Surfers are judged on their ability to perform the most difficult turns on the biggest waves.

54

The Billabong Pro, Tahiti

Held in Teahupoo, Tahiti, the Billabong Pro is part of the men's professional tour.

It involves a group of the 45 top-rated male surfers competing on the world's most challenging waves.

The Billabong Pro, Maui

This is the last event of the women's world tour.

The 17 top-rated female surfers compete for the world title.

The Quiksilver

The Quiksilver is held at Waimea Bay, Hawaii.

It is held when the surf reaches 7.6 metres. In the past 20 years it has only been held six times!

INSPIRATIONAL SURFERS

Kelly Slater is considered the best surfer of all time. Born in Cocoa Beach, Florida, USA, Slater became the youngest-ever world champion at age 20 in 1992.

By 2008, Slater had won a record nine world titles. He has had computer games named after him. Slater is a millionaire.

Kelly Slater statistics

Weight: 72.5 kilograms

Height: 175 centimetres

Stance: Regular
(natural) foot

Australian Layne Beachley is believed to have been the best female professional surfer of all time.

Beachley won a record seventh world title in 2006. In 2008 Layne retired from professional surfing.

Layne Beachley and Kelly Slater

Layne Beachley: statistics

Weight: 55 kilograms

Height: 170 centimetres

Stance: Regular (natural) foot

FOUR FUTURE STARS

Jordy Smith

Jordy Smith is a powerful natural footer from South Africa.

He won a world junior title and is aiming for a world title in the near future.

Adriano de Souza

This Brazilian was named the youngest-ever junior champion when he won the Junior ASP World Championship at age 16.

De Souza is hoping to be the first-ever Brazilian world champion.

Stephanie Gilmore

This Australian won her first-ever professional event, the Quiksilver Pro, at the age of 17.

At the same age, she won her first world championship, the Roxy Pro.

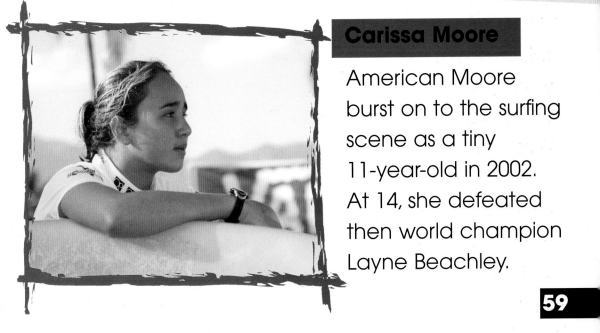

Carissa Moore

American Moore burst on to the surfing scene as a tiny 11-year-old in 2002. At 14, she defeated then world champion Layne Beachley.

MILESTONES

1912 – Hawaii's Duke Kahanamoku wins a gold medal in swimming at the Olympics. Then he travels around the world spreading the word about surfing.

1914 – The first Australian surfer, Isobel Lathem, takes to the water.

1957 – America's Greg Noll surfs Waimea surf spot in Hawaii for the first time. This is considered the start of big-wave surfing.

1966 – Australia's Nat Young wins the world title in California. He's credited with the start of the short-board evolution.

1976 – Peter Townend, from Australia, is crowned the first-ever professional world surfing champion.

1981 – In huge waves at Bells Beach, Australia, Simon Anderson wins the Rip Curl Pro on his new invention, the tri-fin surfboard.

1988 – America's Frieda Zamba sets a new world record by winning her fourth world title.

1992 – Twenty-year-old Kelly Slater is the youngest surfer ever to win a world title.

1998 – On 'Big Thursday', a group of surfers, led by America's Ken Bradshaw, tow surf into the biggest waves ever ridden until that time.

Simon Anderson riding his own invention, the tri-fin, for the first time

Glossary

Big Thursday A famous day of surfing in Hawaii in 1998 when surfers rode the biggest waves (26 metres) in the history of the sport.

Face The open part of a wave that a surfer rides down.

Fibreglass The traditional material that surfboards have been made from since the 1950s.

Goofy footer A surfer that rides with their right foot forward.

Lip The falling top section of a wave.

Pipeline A famous big-wave spot in Hawaii. It is known for its massive tubes. It breaks only 30 metres from shore.

Reef A ridge of sharp rock or coral near the surface of the sea.

Regular footer A surfer that rides with their left foot forward.

Sets Groups of bigger waves that arrive together. Surfers will wait for the sets, as they tend to be the best quality waves.

Take-off The start of surfing a wave when a surfer paddles and is picked up by the force of the wave. Then the surfer jumps to his feet and starts the ride.

Tow surfing A relatively new form of surfing where the surfer is towed into a wave by a powered watercraft or motorized jet ski.

Tri-fin Invented by Australian surfer and surfboard maker, Simon Anderson in 1981, the tri-fin has been the dominant design in surfing ever since.

Tube The ultimate wave in surfing. The curling front part of the wave goes over the surfer, enclosing them inside the wave.

Wave pools Human-made structures that produce waves in large pools.

World junior title Currently held every year in Australia, this is for surfers under 20-years of age.

Index